THE INNER EYE

AWAKENING TO INNER AWARENESS

Author

Bishop Philip Harrison DD, THD

Co-author

Reverend Abraham K. Mulbah, DBS

GIG Publishing, LLC.

Cover design by GIG Publishing, LLC.

Editing and formatting by GIG Publishing, LLC.

Scripture quotations are taken from the ESV and the KJV of the Holy Bible.

This novel is a work of nonfiction.

Printed in the United States of America

ISBN: 979-8-218-67124-2

DEDICATION:

With heartfelt gratitude, I dedicate *The Inner Eye* to those whose unwavering support, wisdom, and contributions have made this work possible. To Rev., Dr. Sam Ndorleh, whose profound insights and guidance have shaped the very essence of this book, your wisdom has been a guiding light. To Rev. Nuhu Toure, my dear friend and brother, whose steadfast encouragement and companionship in faith have strengthened my resolve along this journey. Your presence has been both a blessing and an inspiration.

To Attorney Jack Herzig, whose unwavering encouragement has been a pillar of strength, reminding me that perseverance and belief can overcome any obstacle. And to my beloved daughter, Evangelist Hasha Robertson, whose incredible contributions and devotion to this work have been nothing short of extraordinary. Without each of you, this book would not have been possible. Your faith, support, and love have been instrumental in bringing *The Inner Eye* to life, and for that, I am eternally grateful.

EPIGRAPH:

Within the silence of our own hearts, a wisdom whispers urging us to awaken to the beauty of our inner world.

By: Bishop Philip Harrison DD, Th.D.

Table of Contents

PREFACE:

The human experience is a journey defined by exploration of the world around us and the depths within us. At the heart of this voyage lies the concept of the "inner eye": a profound lens through which we perceive truth, seek wisdom, and connect with the unseen dimensions of existence.

This book, *The Inner Eye*, serves as an invitation to embark on a journey of spiritual discovery and self-awareness. Our modern world, filled with distractions and complexities, often clouds the clarity of our inner vision.

The hustle of daily life can make it easy to overlook the subtle yet significant forces that shape our understanding of purpose, compassion, and interconnectedness.

The chapters of this book are a guide to removing these veils, uncovering insights that illuminate the soul and enrich the mind. This work is not merely a collection of thoughts but a call to reflection and transformation.

It challenges readers to examine the ways in which they perceive themselves, others, and the divine forces that govern creation.

From the power of empathy and compassion to the intricate web of life that binds all living things, the themes within these pages urge us to see beyond the surface, awakening our inner eye to a deeper reality. Each chapter builds upon the next, creating a framework for understanding spiritual truths and their relevance to everyday life. The lessons are drawn from universal principles, bridging wisdom traditions, personal experiences, and contemporary reflections. The aim is to inspire a renewed sense of wonder and responsibility, encouraging readers to live with intentionality and purpose. In a world increasingly in need of connection and understanding, the insights offered here are both timely and timeless.

The Inner Eye allows us to navigate the complexities of existence with clarity, guiding us toward paths of harmony, humility, and gratitude. It reminds us that the greatest journeys are those that lead inward—to a place where truth, love, and enlightenment reside.

This book is dedicated to those who seek to look beyond the physical and touch the essence of their being. May it serve as a companion and guide, offering light in times of uncertainty and a mirror in moments of introspection.

The path to awakening the inner eye is neither easy nor linear, but it is a journey worth undertaking. With gratitude and hope, I invite you to open your heart and mind to the ideas presented in these pages. Let this book be a starting point or a continuation of your spiritual quest, reminding you that the greatest treasures are often hidden in plain sight, waiting to be discovered through the lens of the inner eye.

INTRODUCTION:

Deep within each of us lies a profound source of guidance, wisdom, and knowing. A place where the boundaries of time and space dissolve, and the essence of our true nature is revealed. This is the realm of the inner eye.

For centuries, mystics, sages, and seers have spoken of this inner eye as a gateway to higher states of consciousness, creative insight, and spiritual awakening. It is the seat of our intuition, where the subconscious and conscious minds converge, and the hidden patterns of the universe are made manifest. In the following pages, we invite you to embark on a journey to awaken and illuminate your inner eye.

Through a series of explorations, reflections, and practices, you will discover the secrets of this inner wisdom and learn to trust its guidance. As you delve deeper into the mysteries of the inner eye, you may find that your perception of reality shifts, your creativity and inspiration are unleashed, and your connection to the world around you is transformed forever.

THE INNER EYE

AWAKENING TO INNER AWARENESS

CHAPTER 1:

THE SEEING EYE

In a world where sight is taken for granted, the ability to see is often considered the most basic of senses. People go through their daily lives without giving much thought to the simple act of looking at the world around them.

Yet, for some, this privilege is denied. The gift of sight is not one to be overlooked, for it opens up a world of color, light, and life. The "seeing eye" holds a deeper significance than just the ability to perceive the environment; it is the lens through which we experience and understand our existence.

In this chapter, we will explore the power of sight and the consequences that arise when it is lost. For many, the act of seeing is something so natural, they rarely stop to appreciate it. Imagine waking up in the morning and seeing the sunrise or walking through a park and observing the intricate details of leaves, flowers, and animals. Sight connects us to the world, providing not just the ability to navigate, but also the means to appreciate beauty.

It is through our eyes that we can understand emotions, express ourselves, and communicate with others. The eyes are often referred to as the windows to the soul, as they reflect our deepest feelings and thoughts. Without sight, a person may feel isolated from the vibrant tapestry of the world, unable to engage fully with life's wonders. However, for some, the ability to see is taken away. Whether through disease, injury, or birth defects, losing sight is a profound and life-altering change. The world becomes a blur of shadows and silhouettes, and everyday tasks that were once simple become daunting challenges.

A person who loses their sight must rely on their other senses— hearing, touching, smelling, and even tasting—to navigate their surroundings. Yet, no matter how well these senses compensate, the absence of sight brings a sense of disconnection from the world. This loss not only affects the way a person interacts with their environment but also reshapes their identity and self-perception.

For those who once had the gift of sight, it can be a difficult transition, marked by grief and a profound sense of loss. In the face of such challenges, many who lose their sight embark on a journey of adaptation. The human spirit is resilient, and people who once had vision learn to rely on their other senses to navigate the world. Some people use mobility aids such as canes or guide dogs, while others learn to read braille or use technology designed for the visually impaired. It is a slow and sometimes frustrating process, but many find new ways to experience the world.

The adaptation journey is not just about learning new skills; it is about reshaping one's relationship with the world and finding new avenues of connection. This journey teaches patience, resilience, and the importance of community support. Over time, the visually impaired often develop a heightened awareness of the world through their other senses, finding beauty in sounds, textures, and smells that others may overlook.

One of the most profound ways to assist those who have lost their sight is through the use of guide dogs. These specially trained animals become the eyes for their owners, leading them safely through their daily lives. The bond between a person and their guide dog is unique—built on trust, respect, and mutual understanding.

A seeing-eye dog does not merely follow commands; it responds to the needs of its owner, sensing when the person requires assistance or when danger is near. This partnership allows visually impaired individuals to navigate the world with confidence and independence.

Dogs are trained to lead their owners around obstacles, stop at curbs, and even recognize traffic signals. Through this bond, the "seeing eye" is not just a metaphor, but a living, breathing partner that restores autonomy and dignity to its owner. In addition to guide dogs, modern technology has played a crucial role in helping those who are visually impaired.

Devices such as screen readers, audio books, and smartphone apps have opened up new opportunities for education, work, and entertainment. For example, visually impaired individuals can now listen to news articles, read emails, or navigate websites with ease through the assistance of voice recognition software advent of smart glasses and other wearable technology has made it possible for individuals to receive real-time feedback on their surroundings, providing detailed descriptions of objects and people nearby. Technology has become a vital tool in leveling the playing field, allowing visually impaired individuals to lead fuller lives, connect with others, and engage with the world in ways that were once unimaginable. While the act of seeing through the eyes is often considered the most direct way of experiencing the world, true perception goes beyond what is physically visible.

People who are visually impaired often develop a heightened sensitivity to the world around them, perceiving details that sighted individuals might miss. The ability to hear the subtle rustling of leaves, the scent of rain on the air, or the vibrations of footsteps on the ground allows for a rich sensory experience.

This kind of perception challenges the notion that sight is the most important sense. It teaches us that true vision comes from the mind and heart, allowing individuals to perceive the world not just through their eyes but through a deeper understanding of their surroundings.

Living without sight requires immense courage and determination. It is easy to focus on what is lost, but those who adapt to blindness often discover new strengths within themselves. They develop resilience, problem-solving abilities, and a deeper appreciation for the non-visual aspects of life.

Many individuals who lose their sight go on to accomplish incredible feats— whether it's excelling in careers, creating art, or advocating for the rights of the visually impaired. The absence of sight does not define a person's potential.

In fact, it often becomes a catalyst for self-discovery and personal growth. The courage to live without sight is a testament to the strength of the human spirit and the ability to find new ways of engaging with life, no matter the challenges. The journey of losing and adapting to life without sight is one of transformation. It teaches us that the world is not solely defined by what we can see but by what we can feel, hear, and understand.

The "seeing eye" may perceive the world with a deeper sense of connection. Through guide dogs, technology, and personal resilience, those who lose their sight are able to continue navigating the world, proving that true vision is not just about what is visible to the eye but what is deeply felt within the heart. In the end, the seeing eye is not merely an organ of perception but a symbol of hope, adaptability, and the unyielding power of the human spirit.

CHAPTER 2

THE SPIRITUAL EYES

Our eyes within is the most powerful way God allows us to see His truth nature.

Psalm 119:18 teaches us to ask God to "Open our eyes,

that we may behold wondrous things out of your law".

We will not be able to see the details of God's love without the inner eyes. David was able to see the potential of his ability to defeat Goliath through faith. Even when his brethren tried to discourage him, he saw more than what they were seeing. God has placed in us the potential to have a fulfilled life. Only with the inner eyes you can see this treasure that lies within you.

SEEING YOUR PROBLEMS AND CHALLENGES THROUGH THE INNER EYES

The challenges of life come as an opportunity to see God in a more meaningful way. You must be able to see God in what you encounter daily, see the challenges of life with your spiritual eyes and become the solution that God intends for you.

17

2 Kings 6:17-20

17 Then Elisha prayed and said, "O Lord, please open his eyes that he may see." So, the Lord opened the eyes of the young man, and he saw, and behold, the mountain was full of horses and chariots of fire all around Elisha. 18 And when the Syrians came down against him, Elisha prayed to the Lord and said, "Please strike this people with blindness." So, he struck them with blindness in accordance with the prayer of Elisha. 19 And Elisha said to them, "This is not the way, and this is not the city. Follow me, and I will bring you to the man whom you seek." And he led them to Samaria. 20 As soon as they entered Samaria, Elisha said, "O Lord, open the eyes of these men, that they may see." So, the Lord opened their eyes and they saw, and behold, they were in the midst of Samaria.

The Syrians were depending upon their natural eyes which is only limited to physical things whereas the inner eyes can see both physical and spiritual things. King Nebuchadnezzar saw the fourth man in the fire and his inner eyes immediately realized that this was the son of God. God wants you to see through the inner eyes. There are things that God wants to reveal and show you, but you will not be able to see them through the physical eyes.

Daniel 3:24-25

24 Then Nebuchadnezzar the king was astonished, and rose up in haste, and spoke, and said unto his counsellors, "Didn't we cast three men bound into the midst of the fire?" They answered and said unto the king, True, O king.

25 He answered and said, But, I see four men loose, walking in the midst of the fire, and they have no hurt; and the form of the fourth is like the Son of God.

"The form of the fourth is like the son of God." The King saw the fourth man spiritually and later physically.

There are times God wants you to see whatever you're going through spiritually first, and then, physically. When this is done then we find the solution through the word of God.

God has made provision for whatever we will encounter in our lifetime. Pray that God allows you to see it spiritually

Joshua 1:7-9

7 "Only be thou strong and very courageous, that thou mayest observe to do according to all the law, which Moses my servant commanded thee: turn not from it to the right hand or to the left, that thou mayest prosper wheresoever thou go.

8 This book of the law shall not depart out of thy mouth; but thou shalt meditate therein day and night, that thou mayest observe to do according to all that is written therein: for then thou shalt make thy way prosperous and then thou shalt have good success.

9 Have not I commanded thee? Be strong and of a good courage; be not afraid, neither be thou dismayed: for the Lord thy God is with thee whithersoever thou go.

Peter was able to reveal who Jesus was through the inner eyes:

"Thou are the Christ, the son of the living God." Matthew 16:17.

And Jesus answered him, "Blessed are you, Simon Bar-Jonah! For flesh and blood has not revealed this to you, but my Father who is in heaven.

The phrase "flesh and blood has not revealed" meant that this knowledge was giving by God through Peter's inner eyes (his understanding), that the eyes of your understanding may be enlighten. Spiritual things are never discerned through our physical eyes. These things will be revealed by praying always and asking God to help us by revealing to us those things that will lift up the name of Christ each day of our life.

A child and his parent on a journey to see his grandparent said to his father, "I know how my grandfather looks" and his father replied "you haven't met him how can you say you know how he looks," he replied "because I have seen him through my inner eyes."

Jesus and the two strangers on the road to Emmaus.

Luke 24:13-20

13 Now that same day two of them were going to a village called Emmaus, about seven miles from Jerusalem. 14 They were talking with each other about everything that had happened. 15 As they talked and discussed these things with each other, Jesus himself came up and walked along with them; 16 but they were kept from recognizing him.

17 He asked them, "What are you discussing together as you walk along?"

18 They stood still, their faces downcast. One of them, named Cleopas, asked him, "Are you the only one visiting Jerusalem who does not know the things that have happened there in these days?" 19 "What things?" he asked.

"About Jesus of Nazareth," they replied. "He was a prophet, powerful in word and deed before God and all the people. 20 The chief priests and our rulers handed him over to be sentenced to death, and they crucified him.

While the two were walking on the road to Emmaus, they were preoccupied with the physical and the happening around them, many times when we are focus on the things happening around us, we tend to forget about the spiritual, for the word of God tells us that we do not live by physical sight. The physical sight may mislead us if our spiritual eyes are not in tune with God.

May the Holy Spirit help us to see with our inner eyes, may we not lose track of the things that God has made provision of to help us fulfill purpose in this life. There are opportunities that are made available to us, but you must seize the moment when these opportunities are made available. The bear and the lion were not just obstacles intended to destroy the flock that were entrusted to David, they were intended for David's upliftment, only the inner eyes could see this. On the contrary, natural eyes could have mistaken it for another attack from the enemy.

21

Jeremiah 24:1-3 (KJV)

1 The Lord showed me, and, behold, two baskets of figs were set before the temple of the Lord, after that Nebuchadnezzar king of Babylon had carried away captive Jeconiah the son of Jehoiakim king of Judah, and the princes of Judah, with the carpenters and smiths, from Jerusalem, and had brought them to Babylon.

2 One basket had very good figs, even like the figs that are first ripe: and the other basket had very naughty figs, which could not be eaten, they were so bad.

3 Then said the Lord unto me, What seest thou, Jeremiah? And I said, Figs; the good figs, very good; and the evil, very evil, that cannot be eaten, they are so evil.

What do you see, Jeremiah? God's question to Jeremiah is not merely about physical sight but spiritual insight. The Hebrew word for "see" is "ra'ah," which can mean to perceive or understand. In this passage God was interested in what Jeremiah's perceptions were, not just what were before him at that present time.

Reflect on God's question to Jeremiah for a moment, God may be asking you today; What are you seeing? Don't only see the problems and obstacles but see beyond the impossibilities and great things that you have been enabled to do. Jesus told his disciples "greater things than these shall you do." I declare that may you do greater things today in the name of Jesus, amen and amen. God's intention for you is to fulfill the purpose for which you were created.

Let us pray daily that we will not be spiritually blind.

CHAPTER 3:

WHAT IS A SEEING EYE?

The question, "What is a seeing eye?" goes beyond its literal meaning of vision and delves into the deeper aspects of perception, understanding, and connection. While our physical eyes serve as the primary tool for navigating the world, true sight often involves more than what meets the eye.

The phrase "seeing eye" can symbolize more than just the ability to visually interpret the world; it can represent awareness, insight, and intuition.

In this chapter, we will explore the meaning of a "seeing eye" from various perspectives—its literal interpretation in terms of vision, its metaphorical significance, and its powerful role in guiding those who cannot see through physical means.

The most common interpretation of the "seeing eye" is the one we are all familiar with—the physical organ responsible for vision. Our eyes are not just windows to the world but complex instruments that allow us to perceive light, color, depth, and movement.

They allow us to interact with our surroundings, communicate nonverbally, and make sense of the environment.

The Inner Eye

The seeing eye captures images, processes them through the brain, and helps us make decisions, avoid danger, and enjoy the beauty of the world. In this sense, the seeing eye is the key to our connection to the world around us, and without it, life would be drastically different, limiting not just our activities but also our understanding of existence itself.

Sight plays a fundamental role in shaping our experience of life. It is through our eyes that we engage with the world on a daily basis. We read the faces of those around us to understand their emotions, we enjoy the changing hues of the sky as the day transitions from dawn to dusk, and we navigate spaces by seeing obstacles and finding our way.

Beyond its functional role, sight also influences our emotions and perceptions. Beautiful landscapes, a loved one's smile, or a breathtaking piece of art can evoke powerful feelings, while harsh, frightening, or unfamiliar visuals can trigger fear or anxiety.

The seeing eye thus not only helps us survive but enriches our emotional and aesthetic lives. But what happens when the seeing eye is lost?

For millions of people around the world, blindness or visual impairment is a reality they face each day. Whether it is due to birth defects, accidents, aging, or disease, the absence of sight presents unique challenges.

Individuals who lose their vision must adapt to the world differently, relying on their other senses—hearing, touching, smelling, and tasting—to build a mental map of their surroundings. The seeing eye, in this case, is no longer a physical organ but an internal mechanism that adapts and compensates for the loss of external vision. While these adaptations allow individuals to navigate the world, they also bring forth a new understanding of the world, one that is not solely dependent on sight. Beyond its literal sense, the "seeing eye" can be seen as a metaphor for perception and understanding. It represents not just the physical act of seeing but the deeper capacity to interpret, analyze, and make sense of the world around us.

A seeing eye is not merely one that captures images; it is one that understands and processes those images. In a metaphorical sense, a seeing eye is a mind that perceives beyond the surface, recognizing hidden meanings, uncovering truths, and engaging in critical thinking. This kind of sight is necessary in all walks of life—from interpreting the motivations behind people's actions to understanding complex societal issues.

A person with a "seeing eye" is someone who sees not just what is in front of them but also the unseen patterns that shape the world. The metaphor of the seeing eye also extends into the realm of empathy and emotional intelligence.

A person with a "seeing eye" is often someone who can look beyond the external behaviors and understand the internal struggles of others. They are able to read between the lines, recognize unspoken emotions, and perceive the needs of others without them having to express it explicitly. This deeper form of sight goes beyond physical appearance and includes a profound awareness of others' feelings, desires, and experiences.

The "seeing eye" in this context is a tool for fostering connection and understanding, building relationships based on mutual respect and compassion. It allows individuals to truly "see" one another in ways that transcend the surface-level interactions.

In today's world, technology plays a vital role in assisting those with visual impairments. With advancements in tools such as screen readers, voice activated devices, and navigation aids, the concept of a "seeing eye" has evolved beyond the natural limitations of human sight.

For instance, smartphones equipped with accessibility features now allow individuals to access information, navigate spaces, and even interact with others through audio cues. Additionally, technologies like smart glasses provide real-time descriptions of the environment, helping individuals who cannot see to experience the world in ways that were previously unimaginable.

These technological advancements serve as a modern interpretation of the seeing eye, offering a bridge between the visually impaired and the world around them.

The "seeing eye" also exists in the natural world, where animals have developed unique and extraordinary ways to perceive their surroundings. For example, certain animals, such as bats and dolphins, possess the ability to echolocate, using sound waves to detect objects around them. Similarly, some birds of prey have keen eyesight that allows them to spot small creatures from incredible distances. The animal kingdom offers numerous examples of how different species have developed alternative ways of seeing and navigating the world.

These adaptations highlight the idea that sight is not limited to the human experience and that the concept of a "seeing eye" can extend to the natural world, where various forms of perception are used for survival, communication, and exploration.

In addition to technology, one of the most profound examples of the seeing eye is the guide dog, a loyal companion to those who are blind or visually impaired. A guide dog is trained to be the eyes of its owner, leading them safely through the world and assisting with daily tasks.

These dogs are capable of navigating complex environments, avoiding obstacles, and even recognizing traffic signals to ensure their owners' safety.

The bond between a guide dog and its owner is one of deep trust, as the dog becomes an extension of the person's own perception. In this way, the seeing eye is not only a symbol of independence but also of companionship and mutual support.

In conclusion, the concept of the "seeing eye" encompasses much more than just the ability to see with one's physical eyes.

It represents the myriad ways in which we perceive, understand, and interact with the world around us. Whether it is the literal sense of sight, the metaphorical ability to see deeper truths, or the technological and animal-assisted tools that help us navigate the world, the seeing eye plays a crucial role in shaping our lives. It teaches us that sight is not merely about vision but about perception, understanding, and connection.

The seeing eye, in all its forms, invites us to expand our awareness, enhance our empathy, and find new ways to experience the world in all its complexity.

CHAPTER 4:

WHO SEES?

The act of seeing is often considered a simple and natural process: light enters the eye, is processed by the brain, and voilà, we perceive the world around us. But the question "Who sees?" challenges this simplistic view. Is it only those who are physically capable of seeing? Or does the term "seeing" extend beyond the literal sense to encompass deeper, more subjective forms of perception?

In this chapter, we will explore the idea of who truly sees—both in the literal sense of vision and in the broader, metaphorical sense. We will examine the ways in which people perceive the world and how various factors, such as personal experience, emotional intelligence, and even culture, influence our understanding of what it means to "see."

At its most basic, the ability to see is attributed to those who possess functional eyes and the necessary cognitive systems to process visual stimuli. Sight allows individuals to interpret their surroundings, react to danger, and navigate through their environment. For many people, seeing is a straightforward process: they look, and they understand what they are observing.

The Inner Eye

This form of seeing is integral to our daily lives, enabling us to recognize faces, read books, watch television, and interact with others. Without the ability to see, life would become more challenging, as visual cues often guide our actions and decisions. In this sense, those with physical sight are the primary "seers" of the world, interpreting it through the lens of their eyes.

But what about those who cannot see? Are they excluded from the act of "seeing"? Not at all. Blind individuals may not experience the world visually, but they often possess a heightened sense of other forms of perception—touch, hearing, smell, and intuition. People who are blind or visually impaired have developed extraordinary skills to navigate their surroundings, relying on a complex interplay of their other senses to fill the gap left by the absence of sight. Blindness forces them to "see" the world in different ways, tuning in more closely to sounds, textures, and vibrations.

These individuals may also develop a deeper emotional awareness, interpreting the world through their feelings and instincts.

In this sense, the blind are "seers" in a unique, nuanced way, one that goes beyond traditional sight. Beyond external perception lies the "inner sight"—the ability to look within and understand one's own thoughts, emotions, and motivations. This kind of seeing is about introspection, self-awareness, and emotional intelligence. Some people have a remarkable ability to "see" themselves clearly, understanding their strengths, weaknesses, and desires. This inner sight is often cultivated through reflection, mindfulness, and experiences of personal growth.

It enables individuals to make informed decisions, recognize unhealthy patterns, and develop a deeper understanding of their relationships with others. The inner seer is not concerned with the world outside but with the world within, seeking clarity, truth, and personal development. Another form of seeing comes through emotional individuals, interpreting their surroundings, react to danger, and navigate through their environment. For many people, seeing is a straightforward process: they look, and they understand what they are observing. This form of seeing is integral to our daily lives, enabling us to recognize faces, read books, watch television, and interact with others.

Without the ability to see, life would become more challenging, as visual cues often guide our actions and decisions. In this sense, those with physical sight are the primary "seers" of the world, interpreting it through the lens of their eyes. But what about those who cannot see?

Are they excluded from the act of "seeing"? Not at all. Blind individuals may not experience the world visually, but they often possess a heightened sense of other forms of perception—touch, hearing, smell, and intuition. People who are blind or visually impaired have developed extraordinary skills to navigate their surroundings, relying on a complex interplay of their other senses to fill the gap left by the absence of sight.

The Inner Eye

Blindness forces them to "see" the world in different ways, tuning in more closely to sounds, textures, and vibrations. These individuals may also develop a deeper emotional awareness, interpreting the world through their feelings and instincts. In this sense, the blind are "seers" in a unique, nuanced way; one that goes beyond traditional sight. Beyond external perception lies the "inner sight"—the ability to look within and understand one's own thoughts, emotions, and motivations.

This kind of seeing is about introspection, self-awareness, and emotional intelligence. Some people have a remarkable ability to "see" themselves clearly, understanding their strengths, weaknesses, and desires. This inner sight is often cultivated through reflection, mindfulness, and experiences of personal growth.

It enables individuals to make informed decisions, recognize unhealthy patterns, and develop a deeper understanding of their relationships with others. The inner seer is not concerned with the world outside but with the world within, seeking clarity, truth, and personal development. Another form of seeing comes through emotional intelligence and empathy—the ability to understand the emotions, needs, and experiences of others. The emotional seer is not just aware of what others feel but can often sense it before it is expressed in words.

This deep form of seeing involves tuning into nonverbal cues such as body language, facial expressions, and tone of voice. It requires a heightened awareness of how others are feeling and the ability to interpret these feelings in context.

Empathy allows individuals to connect on a deeper level, creating meaningful relationships and understanding. The emotional seer can "see" into the hearts of others, even when they are not able to articulate their feelings fully.

Our ability to "see" is also influenced by the cultures we are born into and the experiences we have throughout our lives. Each culture has its own way of interpreting the world, shaping how individuals perceive their environment and their place within it.

The cultural seer understands the nuances of these social constructs and how they affect perceptions of identity, race, gender, and other societal factors. In many ways, our cultural background acts as a lens through which we "see" the world and interact with others. What one culture may view as normal or beautiful, another may consider strange or offensive.

This broader understanding of who sees helps us recognize that vision is not just an individual process but a collective one, shaped by the societies we belong to. In many philosophical and spiritual traditions, "seeing" extends beyond the material world into the realm of the divine or transcendent.

The spiritual seer is someone who perceives beyond the physical senses and connects with higher truths or the essence of existence. Whether through meditation, prayer, or altered states of consciousness, spiritual seers claim to have access to deeper layers of reality that are not visible to the ordinary eye.

These individuals often speak of visions, revelations, or a sense of oneness with the universe, which others may find difficult to understand or accept.

The spiritual seer represents the ultimate quest for enlightenment, seeking to see the world as it truly is, beyond the distractions and illusions of the physical plane. In today's world, technology has altered the way we "see" and experience the world.

With the advent of artificial intelligence, virtual reality, and augmented reality, the very concept of sight has expanded beyond biological limitations.

Machines now "see" through sensors, cameras, and algorithms, providing insights into areas that were previously inaccessible to human perception. For example, self-driving cars can navigate roads using complex visual recognition software, while AI systems can analyze vast amounts of data to detect patterns that humans might miss.

The technological seer represents a new frontier in perception, one where machines assist in human vision or even surpass it in some cases. This raises important questions about what it means to "see" in the age of artificial intelligence.

Finally, the collective seer refers to the power of community and collaboration in shaping perception. When individuals come together with a shared vision or purpose, they are able to "see" solutions and possibilities that may not have been apparent to them alone. Collective action has the power to create societal change, spark innovation, and address global challenges. Movements for civil rights, environmental justice, and equality all began with a group of people "seeing" the world differently and working together to make it better.

The collective seer highlights the importance of collaboration and unity in bringing about positive change, showing that vision is not always about individual insight but about the collective wisdom that emerges when people join forces. In conclusion, the question "Who sees?" reveals the complexity of perception and the many ways in which individuals interpret the world. While physical sight remains one of the primary ways we interact with our environment, the ability to see goes far beyond the limits of the eyes.

Emotional intelligence, cultural awareness, spiritual insight, technological advancements, and collective action all shape how we perceive and engage with the world. Whether through empathy, introspection, or a shared vision, there are many forms of seeing that extend beyond the physical act of looking.

As we explore and understand these various ways of seeing, we begin to realize that true vision is not limited to the eyes but is a broader, more nuanced process that involves the mind, heart, and spirit.

CHAPTER 5:

WHAT IS THE SPIRITUAL

MEANING OF SEER?

Throughout history, the concept of the "seer" has captured the imaginations of many across different cultures and spiritual traditions. A seer is often considered someone who possesses extraordinary perception—someone who can look beyond the physical world and glimpse deeper truths about existence. But what is the spiritual meaning of a seer?

Is a seer merely a prophet or a mystic, or is the role more nuanced and complex? In this chapter, we will explore the spiritual significance of being a seer, examining how this ability transcends physical sight and enters the realm of higher consciousness, divine connection, and spiritual awakening.

At the core of the spiritual meaning of a seer is the idea that they serve as a conduit for divine wisdom. In many spiritual traditions, a seer is believed to possess the ability to receive insights directly from the divine or the universe.

This can manifest in various forms—visions, dreams, intuitive knowing, or even a deep inner sense of truth. These experiences are not simply the result of personal insight but are understood as messages from a higher power, spirit guides, or the collective consciousness. The seer, therefore, plays a vital role in bringing divine wisdom to the physical world, offering guidance, direction, and understanding to those who seek it. One of the most recognized aspects of the spiritual seer is clairvoyance, or the ability to perceive events, situations, or truths that are hidden from ordinary view. While physical sight allows us to see the material world, the seer's gift of clairvoyance allows them to access higher realms of reality. This ability to "see beyond" is not limited to time or space, and many seers report receiving insights about the past, present, and future.

Clairvoyance, in a spiritual sense, is often viewed as a gift that comes with responsibility, as it can bring great insight but also requires discernment to interpret these visions correctly. Seers use their clairvoyance not only to understand the world on a deeper level but to guide others in their spiritual journeys.

A crucial element of the spiritual meaning of the seer is their connection to the inner realms of consciousness. The ability to "see" spiritually is often linked to an elevated state of awareness, where the boundaries between the conscious mind, the unconscious mind, and the spiritual realms become porous.

Seers are believed to have access to these higher planes, where they can receive information that is not available in ordinary waking life. This connection to the inner realms requires deep meditative practices, self-awareness, and an openness to the unseen. Through this heightened state of awareness, seers can access profound insights that guide their actions and the actions of those around them.

In many spiritual traditions, the seer is also considered a healer. The act of seeing is not limited to the mind's eye but extends to the spirit and the body. Through their heightened perception, seers can identify imbalances, blockages, or energies that may be preventing healing or spiritual growth in others. This ability to sense the unseen, whether it be physical illness, emotional distress, or spiritual dissonance, allows seers to offer healing on multiple levels.

The seer's healing process may involve energy work, spiritual counseling, or channeling divine wisdom to help individuals restore balance and alignment with their true self. In this way, the seer is not only a witness to the spiritual world but an active participant in the healing and transformation of others.

Intuition plays a significant role in the life of a seer. While clairvoyance may provide visions or glimpses of truth, it is often the seer's deep intuitive sense that guides them in interpreting and acting upon these insights. Spiritual seers are highly attuned to their intuitive senses, which allow them to "feel" the truth of a situation even before it becomes clear in the material world.

This intuition is often described as a "knowing" that comes without reasoning, a sudden flash of insight that feels undeniable. For many seers, trusting their intuition is as important as their ability to receive visions, as it allows them to navigate the complexities of the spiritual realm and make decisions that align with their highest purpose.

The path of the seer is often one that requires a delicate balance between light and darkness. Spiritual vision is not always about receiving uplifting or positive messages; sometimes, the seer must confront the shadow side of the self and the world. Seers are often called to see truths that others may not want to face— the pain, the suffering, and the injustices that exist within society or the human soul. This dark aspect of being a seer is a necessary part of the journey, as it allows for growth, transformation, and healing.

By confronting the darkness, the seer becomes a beacon of light, helping others navigate their own shadows and move toward spiritual enlightenment.

One of the most important aspects of the spiritual meaning of the seer is their role as a guide for others on their spiritual journeys. Seers are often sought out for their wisdom, insight, and ability to offer clarity in times of confusion.

Because of their unique ability to perceive the hidden aspects of reality, they are in a position to help others understand their own lives and spiritual paths. The seer serves as a mirror, reflecting back the truths that may be difficult for others to see on their own.

By offering guidance, encouragement, and sometimes warnings, the seer plays a pivotal role in helping others find their way toward spiritual awakening, healing, and growth. Becoming a spiritual seer is often not a choice but a calling.

It is a journey that requires dedication, practice, and the willingness to embrace the unknown. The path to awakening one's spiritual vision is often fraught with challenges, as it requires letting go of preconceived notions and attachments to the physical world. A seer's journey is one of inner transformation, where they must confront their own fears, doubts, and limitations in order to access higher states of consciousness. It is a process of surrendering to the divine and trusting in the wisdom that flows through them.

As they continue on this path, they deepen their connection to the spiritual realms, strengthening their ability to see with clarity and purpose. In conclusion, the spiritual meaning of a seer is one of profound insight, responsibility, and connection to the divine.

The seer is not simply someone who can predict the future or offer glimpses of unseen worlds; they are individuals who have awakened to a higher state of perception and consciousness. Through their connection to divine wisdom, clairvoyance, intuition, and healing abilities, seers serve as guides, teachers, and light bearers for others.

They help illuminate the path of spiritual growth, offering clarity and insight that transcend the limitations of the physical senses. The role of the seer, therefore, is not just to see the world differently, but to help others see the truth and beauty that lies hidden beneath the surface of reality.

CHAPTER 6:

THE EYE THAT SEES.

The eye is often referred to as the window to the soul, a metaphor that suggests a deep connection between physical vision and the inner workings of the human spirit.

While the physical eye is responsible for processing light and allowing us to see the material world, there exists a deeper kind of sight that transcends what is visible to the naked eye. In this chapter, we will explore the concept of the "eye that sees" as it relates not only to physical vision but to spiritual sight, intuition, and perception.

This broader understanding of the eye expands the notion of sight, guiding us to consider how we perceive the world around us on multiple levels: emotionally, mentally, and spiritually. At its most basic level, the eye is a highly complex organ that allows humans to perceive the world around them.

Through light, the eyes capture images and send them to the brain for interpretation. In this sense, the physical eye functions as a tool, a highly sophisticated mechanism that helps humans navigate their surroundings, detect danger, and engage with the world. The eye is not simply a passive receiver of light; it actively processes visual information, enabling us to see colors, shapes, textures, and movement. This primary sense of sight plays an essential role in human survival and experience. Without it, our interaction with the world would be drastically different, making the eye indispensable to our everyday lives. In many cultures and spiritual traditions, the eye is not just a biological organ but a symbol of knowledge and enlightenment.

The "all-seeing eye" is often associated with higher wisdom, a deeper understanding that goes beyond the superficial. It represents the ability to see the truth, to look beyond appearances, and to perceive the underlying reality of the world.

This symbolic use of the eye connects sight to awareness, suggesting that to truly "see" is to understand not just what is in front of us, but the deeper meaning and connections behind what we observe.

In this way, the eye that sees is also a metaphor for clarity of mind and consciousness. One of the most profound concepts related to the "eye that sees" is the notion of the "third eye," a term often used in spiritual contexts to refer to the inner eye or spiritual sight.

This metaphorical eye is believed to be located in the middle of the forehead, between the eyebrows, and is said to be responsible for perceiving spiritual truths and higher states of consciousness. The third eye is associated with intuition, wisdom, and the ability to perceive beyond the material world. Cultivating this inner vision is thought to lead to a deeper understanding of reality, where individuals can access truths that are not immediately visible to the physical eye. This "eye" allows people to connect with higher realms of consciousness and explore the mysteries of existence in ways that go beyond ordinary perception. Intuition is often described as the "eye" that sees the truth without needing explicit evidence or logical reasoning. It is an innate sense of knowing that arises from within, guiding individuals in ways that are not always explainable through conventional means. This type of sight is not based on sensory input but rather on an inner wisdom or feeling that guides us toward a deeper understanding of a situation or person.

The intuitive eye does not need words or explanations to "see" the truth; it simply knows. This intuitive perception often plays a critical role in decision-making, allowing individuals to navigate complex situations with a sense of certainty that transcends rational thought.

It is the ability to see the unseen and understand what is not immediately apparent.

The "eye that sees" also extends into the realm of emotional and compassionate perception. Compassion is often described as the ability to see the world through the eyes of another, understanding their pain, joy, and struggles as if they were your own.

This deeper form of seeing involves not just empathy but a genuine connection with others, where the observer perceives the world from the heart, rather than through the lens of judgment or detachment.

The eye of compassion allows individuals to see beyond surface level appearances, recognizing the humanity in others and the shared experiences that bind us all.

By cultivating this form of sight, individuals can foster greater understanding, healing, and connection. The eye of the mind refers to our ability to process information, analyze situations, and think critically about the world. This type of sight is associated with intellectual perception, the mental clarity required to see through confusion and make informed decisions. The eye of the mind allows individuals to observe patterns, make connections, and discern meaning from complex ideas or situations.

In the age of information overload, the ability to see clearly with the mind is more important than ever.

It involves cultivating mental discipline, focus, and the ability to filter out distractions to see the essential truths that lie hidden beneath layers of noise and confusion.

The eye of the soul is the deepest and most profound level of perception, one that connects us to the divine and to the spiritual essence of all things. It is through the eye of the soul that individuals can experience oneness with the universe, see the interconnectedness of all life, and tap into a universal source of wisdom. This kind of seeing is often described as transcending the limitations of the ego and individual self, allowing the person to perceive the unity of existence.

The eye of the soul opens the individual to experiences of love, peace, and enlightenment, and it is often through this eye that one can access spiritual experiences such as moments of deep insight, epiphanies, or even mystical visions. The concept of the "eye that sees" is not just limited to personal perception but also extends to those who have the ability to interpret these deeper levels of sight— seers. Seers are individuals who can access these layers of spiritual, intuitive, and compassionate perception and offer guidance to others. Whether through prophecy, healing, or spiritual counseling, the role of the seer is to help others understand what their own "eyes" may not yet be able to see. A seer is a guide who can translate the messages of the unseen into practical wisdom, helping others navigate their paths and connect with higher truths. The seer's ability to see the invisible is a gift that often comes with great responsibility, as it involves helping others see their own truths, even when they are hidden beneath layers of doubt or fear. In conclusion, the "eye that sees" is a multifaceted concept that transcends the limitations of physical sight.

While the physical eye plays a crucial role in helping us navigate the material world, the deeper "eyes" within—such as the third eye, the eye of compassion, the eye of the mind, and the eye of the soul—offer a more holistic and enriched vision of reality.

The Inner Eye

These eyes allow us to see not only the surface but also the deeper layers of existence, to perceive truths that lie beyond appearances, and to connect with others and the divine in profound ways. The journey toward awakening the eye that sees is one of spiritual growth, self-awareness, and openness to the unseen. It is a path of discovering deeper wisdom, love, and unity, and through this expanded vision, we can live more fully and consciously, embracing all aspects of our being.

CHAPTER 7:

THE EYE THAT LOOKS

While the concept of sight is often associated with the act of seeing, there is a subtle yet significant difference between seeing and looking. Seeing is the passive reception of light through the eyes, but looking requires active engagement and intention. The eye that looks is more than a sensory organ—it is a tool of focus, will, and purpose. In this chapter, we will explore what it means to look, not just physically, but emotionally, mentally, and spiritually.

Looking implies a deeper level of attention, curiosity, and intention, making it an essential component of understanding, growth, and transformation. Looking, in its simplest form, is the act of directing one's attention toward something. However, it is not just about the direction of gaze but the quality of that attention.

To truly "look" at something involves focusing on it, taking the time to observe its details, and immersing oneself in the experience of seeing. Unlike passive seeing, looking demands a conscious effort. It requires us to slow down, tune in, and be present.

The Inner Eye

This focused attention allows us to engage with our environment on a deeper level, transforming an ordinary experience into an opportunity for learning, discovery, and connection. The eye that looks is deeply connected to the way we engage with the external world.

When we look at the world around us, we are interacting with our surroundings on a physical, sensory level. However, the eye that looks does more than just scan the environment—it is a gateway to understanding.

When we look at nature, we see not just the beauty of the trees and the sky but the interconnections of life, the cycle of seasons, and the wisdom embedded in the natural world. Similarly, when we look at other people, we do more than glance at their appearance; we have the potential to notice their emotions, intentions, and deeper layers of identity. Looking, therefore, invites us to be present with the world and opens the door to deeper understanding.

While the eye that looks is often associated with external perception, it is just as important when we turn our gaze inward. Looking within involves self- reflection, introspection, and the courage to face one's inner world.

This type of looking asks us to observe our thoughts, emotions, and desires without judgment, helping us to understand our inner workings and motivations. The eye that looks inward allows us to access the deeper layers of the subconscious mind, where hidden beliefs, fears, and wounds reside.

The Inner Eye

By looking within, we begin the process of self-awareness and healing, which are essential steps toward spiritual growth and transformation. Looking is an essential tool for learning, as it allows us to absorb new information and make sense of the world. In the educational process, the act of looking is fundamental to understanding complex ideas, solving problems, and developing skills. It is through looking that we observe patterns, identify connections, and make decisions. Whether we are learning a new language, mastering a craft, or exploring a new area of knowledge, looking enables us to gather the necessary data to form insights. This active form of attention enhances our ability to engage with new material, retain information, and integrate it into our existing understanding.

At a deeper level, looking also involves the search for meaning. It is not enough to merely look at something; we often look for something more—answers, insights, significance. This searching gaze is a core part of the human experience. In times of hardship or uncertainty, individuals may look for meaning in their struggles, trying to understand the lessons hidden within adversity.

Similarly, when faced with beauty or joy, we may look for the deeper significance of these moments. Looking for meaning is a spiritual quest, as it involves seeking purpose and understanding in all aspects of life. The eye that looks for meaning is driven by the desire to uncover the truths that lie beneath the surface, whether in the context of personal growth, relationships, or the mysteries of existence. Looking is not just about observing; it is also a way of connecting with others.

When we look at people, we have the opportunity to engage with their experiences, emotions, and perspectives. Empathy—the ability to understand and share the feelings of another—is deeply linked to the act of looking. Through compassionate looking, we can see beyond surface-level appearances and connect with others on a deeper level. This form of looking allows us to recognize the shared humanity in others, fostering relationships built on mutual understanding and respect.

The eye that looks with empathy becomes a bridge between individuals, creating space for compassion, communication, and connection. One of the most powerful aspects of the eye that looks is its ability to see beyond surface appearances.

The world around us is often filled with distractions, judgments, and superficial impressions that obscure the truth. However, when we look beyond the surface, we begin to understand the deeper essence of things.

Looking beyond the surface involves questioning assumptions, challenging stereotypes, and moving beyond first impressions.

This deeper form of looking allows us to see the layers of complexity in people, situations, and experiences. It helps us uncover hidden truths and understand that things are often more intricate and multifaceted than they first appear. Looking also involves the ability to gaze into the future, envisioning possibilities and potential outcomes.

This forward-looking perspective is essential for planning, goalsetting, and personal growth. When we look toward the future, we are engaging with our hopes, dreams, and aspirations. We imagine what could be, based on the decisions we make today.

The eye that looks toward the future enables us to set a direction for our lives, to create vision and purpose. It encourages us to look beyond the limitations of the present moment and strive toward growth, improvement, and positive change. In conclusion, the eye that looks is far more than a passive sense organ.

It is a dynamic and purposeful tool that allows us to engage with the world on multiple levels—physically, emotionally, mentally, and spiritually. The act of looking involves focus, intention, and curiosity, whether we are looking outward at the world or inward at ourselves. Looking enables us to learn, connect, seek meaning, and uncover deeper truths.

It invites us to look beyond the surface and explore the complexity of life, to approach others with empathy, and to envision the possibilities of the future. By cultivating the eye that looks, we transform our ability to interact with the world, to grow, and to discover the hidden layers of existence. Through conscious and intentional looking, we open ourselves to greater understanding, connection, and transformation.

CHAPTER 8:

PHYSICAL BLINDNESS

Physical blindness is defined as the eyes that cannot see any natural image and cannot be corrected by any medical means; it is also referred to as the light of the body. God gave us eyes for us to see and appreciate the wonderful works the Lord has given us and to benefit from it as well. Therefore, if anyone loses this precious gift of God (eyesight), that God has given us, it's considered a loss of vision or physically blind.

PHYSICAL BLINDNESS AT WORK

My motivational inspiration for developing the thoughts and the title of this book, "The Inner Eye: Awakening to Inner Awareness," is because I am blind and have come across blind individuals who have exceptionally unique, inner eyes abilities-confronting many challenges associated with work and fitting in the society of competitive world of vigor.

The places I worked and schools attended, are places where one will experience blindness at work which reveals or exposes a great amount of tremendous diversity of potentials in combination with the divine gift of the inner eyes. However, there is an inner eyes ability exhibited in the context of hands-on work which is miraculously enhanced and the capability of accurately operating machines, electronics and other equipment, truly exposes the in-built inner eyes potentials stored in blindness, therefore the theology of blindness in the context of apocalyptic combinations narratives is hereby revealed through the inner eyes. Sufferers of physical blindness have an inner eyes ability to do an exploit when testifying to the truth that physical blindness is not a limitation to one's progress.

To be spiritually blind is more dangerous than to be physically blind. Being unable to discern the things that are of the spirit of God, and therefore, leaves peoples into the perception of the reality of the rue image or, the ultimate destiny of natural blindness along with its theology, is actually complex in definition, relative to spiritual alliance. It tells us that one can be physically blind but spiritually sighted and can perform and see spiritual things.

There are different types of physical blindness. The one that is commonly associated with us is the loss of eyesight, but there are other blindnesses.

However, beyond the initial perception of loss, there are deeper layers of understanding and significance related to blindness. While society typically views blindness as a limitation, many who experience it describe a unique journey of adaptation, resilience, and profound insight. In this chapter, we will explore the nature of physical blindness, how it affects individuals both practically and emotionally, and how it shapes one's relationship with the world. This chapter aims to break down the misconceptions and show that blindness is not merely a loss but a different way of engaging with reality.

Physical blindness results from a variety of causes, ranging from genetic conditions to accidents, disease, or aging. The science behind blindness can vary significantly depending on the condition. For example, congenital blindness occurs when a person is born without the ability to see, while acquired blindness develops later in life, often as a result of trauma, disease (such as cataracts, glaucoma, or macular degeneration), or injury to the eyes or optic nerves. The brain relies on a complex network of eyes, nerves, and neurons to process visual information, so when this system is disrupted— whether by damage to the eyes or the pathways to the brain—the result is blindness. Understanding these mechanisms is important for understanding the physical and emotional impact of blindness. The emotional journey of blindness varies from person to person, depending on the onset of blindness, the age at which it occurs, and the individual's coping mechanisms.

For many, the loss of sight can lead to a period of grief, as the ability to see is such a significant part of human experience. The loss of visual perception can be deeply disorienting, and it can trigger feelings of isolation, fear, and helplessness.

It is common for those who lose their sight later in life to experience a sense of mourning for the world they can no longer visually engage with. However, as time passes, many individuals find ways to adapt, using their other senses to fill in the gaps left by their loss. Learning to navigate the world through sound, touch, and even intuition can bring a sense of empowerment and new perspectives. One of the most challenging aspects of physical blindness is the social stigma and misconceptions that surround it. People who are blind are often perceived as helpless or dependent, but this assumption is far from the truth.

In reality, blind individuals often develop heightened abilities in other senses, such as hearing and touch, allowing them to navigate the world in ways that those with sight cannot. Despite this, societal attitudes can still be a barrier. There are prevalent stereotypes that blind people cannot lead full, independent lives or participate in activities that sighted people take for granted. This can lead to feelings of frustration, alienation, and the need to constantly prove their abilities to others. Challenging these misconceptions is crucial in helping blind individuals achieve acceptance and integration into society.

Assistive technology has revolutionized the way blind individuals interact with the world. From braille books and tactile maps to screen readers and voice recognition software, technology has provided countless tools that make daily tasks more manageable. For example, text to-speech software enables blind people to read documents, browse the internet, and communicate more easily. Modern advancements, like GPS systems designed specifically for the blind, allow for greater independence in navigating public spaces.

The Inner Eye

These technologies do not just make life easier; they empower individuals to pursue careers, education, and leisure activities that would have otherwise been difficult or impossible. The role of assistive technology in reducing the barriers imposed by physical blindness cannot be overstated. While blindness may seem like a limitation, many blind individuals report that losing their sight allows them to gain deeper insight into life. The absence of sight often prompts a shift in focus from the external world to the internal one. In the absence of visual stimuli, people often find themselves relying more on their other senses, their emotions, and their intuition. Many blind individuals have described a heightened sense of awareness in their other senses, such as hearing, touch, and smell. This expanded perception often leads to greater mindfulness and a deeper connection to the environment and people around them. Blindness, in this sense, is not just a physical condition; it can be a transformative experience that opens new doors to perception and spiritual insight.

The blind community has long been a source of support, camaraderie, and empowerment for those who live with blindness. Support groups, advocacy organizations, and social networks have become essential for blind individuals, providing not just practical assistance but emotional and social connections.

These networks help individuals share experiences, learn coping strategies, and fight for equal rights and opportunities. Whether through online forums, local meet ups, or national organizations, blind people can find a sense of belonging and solidarity. These communities also serve as powerful advocates, working to challenge societal perceptions of blindness and push for greater accessibility in all areas of life, including transportation, education, and employment. Education and employment are two areas where individuals with blindness face significant challenges, but also opportunities for success.

With the right tools and support, blind individuals can pursue higher education and careers, often excelling in fields that require creativity, critical thinking, and specialized knowledge. Many universities and employers are increasingly adopting inclusive policies that provide accommodations for blind students and employees.

Specialized services, such as accessible course materials, adaptive technology, and on-the-job support, allow blind individuals to participate fully in academic and professional environments. While barriers still exist, the progress made in the inclusion of blind individuals in education and employment continues to grow, fostering greater independence and empowerment.

For many individuals who are blind, their blindness does not define them—it is simply one aspect of their identity. Blindness, like any other characteristic, can be integrated into a broader sense of self.

People who are blind may have passions, dreams, and goals, just as sighted individuals do. Embracing blindness as a part of who they are, rather than something to be ashamed of or feared, allows individuals to live more fully and authentically. Blindness can become a powerful part of their personal narrative, contributing to their resilience, resourcefulness, and empathy.

Through the acceptance of their condition, many blind individuals develop a strong sense of identity and pride in their ability to thrive in a world that often views their disability as a limitation.

In conclusion, physical blindness, while often perceived as a loss, can also be an opportunity for growth, transformation, and deeper understanding. Blindness challenges individuals to engage with the world in new ways, relying on senses and skills that are often overlooked by those with sight. Through the use of assistive technologies, strong community networks, and an empowered mindset, blind individuals can navigate the world with independence, dignity, and success.

Rather than viewing blindness as a barrier, it can be seen as a unique lens through which individuals gain insight into life, cultivating resilience, empathy, and an expanded perception of reality. The experience of physical blindness, when reframed, has the potential to lead to profound personal and collective growth.

Moreover, there are many accounts of individuals in the secular world and from a biblical standpoint who triumph in their season of darkness as they battled with this life altering illness- "Physical Blindness or visual impairment".

A famous American author by the name of Helen Keller was known best for overcoming such adversities. She makes us aware that victory is indeed a mindset. From a biblical context, Victory has already been given unto us as believers and children of the most high God. For we are no longer fighting for victory but fighting from victory.

For one to be a victor or remain "Victorious" is often contingent upon one's ability to renew their mind about such life altering events.

Furthermore, Helen Keller became deaf and blind as a toddler due to a febrile illness. Some researchers and biographies concluded that her blindness derived out of the cold hands of rubella, meningitis and scarlet fever or something alike. Although, young Keller's life was interrupted by such life altering disabilities at a very tender age, Keller's optimism and drive to persevere through the storms of life allowed her to overcome such limitations, that wanted to leave her physically and emotionally handicap.

Keller was able to triumph and dance through the rain of life by looking past the natural, into the supernatural. One of her famous quotes is, "The only thing worse than being blind is having sight but no vision". Throughout Helen Keller's life, she painted a visual imagery through her life achievements, that vision is far more important than the ability to see. Keller's quote provides great insight, that lacking vision is one of the primary assassins to living a life of fulfillment, meaning and purpose. Vision goes beyond one's ability to see, but it overflows into our ability to dream, create goals and discover our purpose for existing. It is vision that gives birth to hope and self-discovery.

"I have realized in my own personal life that my greatest art and creative nature was often cultivated by some sort of limitation. Being limited in one area often stirs up your gifts and talents in other areas."

-Evangelist Hasha Robertson

Helen Keller's life has truly created awareness that we are not limited or defined by our circumstances. Mrs. Keller's life has provided great reference for those who are physically blind as well as individuals who have their physical sight but are spiritually impaired or spiritually blind. Helen Keller's life has truly created awareness that we are not limited or defined by our circumstances.

EVANGELIST HASHA STATES:

"As a woman and child of God, embodied with the Holy Spirit, "The sustainer and giver of life, which is an empowerment agent that was given as a gift to all believers of Jesus Christ". The Holy Spirit is a gift that enables one to navigate through the vicissitudes of life. It empowers us to overcome life challenges and live a life of resilience.

Over the years, I have also seen such characteristics and attributes perpetuated and embedded in my father, Bishop Dr. Philip K. Harrison. His zeal, passion and desire to champion the quality of life has truly been inspiring to everyone who crosses his path. Although some day Bishop's hands may grow faint and his spirit down cast due to the absence of his physical sight. He always manages to rise above the clouds. He is indeed my "Hero". I have witnessed him navigate through life's transitions, overcoming every hurled and bypassing roadblock that came to hinder or slow him down. I say, it can only be God's grace and favor that has located such a man.

Bishop's life has indeed fulfilled the scriptures. The Lord has transformed his disadvantages and made them an advantage. He took his weakness and made him strong and took his fears and granted him courage.

Waking up every morning with a new task and goal in mind has been my father's, Bishop Philip Harrison's, daily epistle. He sees life challenges as a podium to announce and unlock another level of God's grace and mercies. He rises every day and laughs at his adversities. For it is written, "For what doesn't kill you, only makes you stronger."

Daddy, I just want to use this platform to express my love and admiration for you. I can't even imagine my life without you, with tears rolling down my face; I just want to say thank you for all your sacrifices for our family, me and the entire body of Christ. Everything about your life signifies that God has indeed called you as a sign and a wonder to impact your generation and generations to come. Your legacy will not die but live and bring light to a lost and dark world. May the grace and hand of God continue to rest firmly upon you and grant you everlasting peace.

In Jesus Mighty name". -Credited to my daughter -Evangelist

Hasha Robertson

CHAPTER 9:

SPIRITUAL BLINDNESS

Spiritual blindness is not merely the absence of sight but the inability to perceive truth, wisdom, and the divine reality.

Unlike physical blindness, which affects the eyes, spiritual blindness clouds the soul and mind, preventing individuals from recognizing the profound truths that govern life.

This condition often leads to misguided priorities, moral confusion, and a detachment from one's higher purpose. Understanding spiritual blindness is essential for navigating the complexities of life with clarity and purpose. Spiritual blindness often stems from a variety of internal and external factors.

Personal pride, materialism, and an over-reliance on human reasoning can obstruct spiritual insight. External influences such as societal norms, misinformation, and toxic relationships can also play a role. A spiritually blind person may exhibit several key symptoms, such as a lack of empathy, persistent dissatisfaction, and an inability to discern right from wrong. Such individuals may focus solely on material success while neglecting relationships, moral responsibilities, or personal growth. They might also reject wisdom, resist change, and find it difficult to grasp the importance of faith or spiritual practices. Spiritual blindness can severely impact personal and communal relationships.

It often breeds selfishness, misunderstanding, and conflict. Those who are spiritually blind may struggle to see the needs of others or to recognize their own shortcomings, leading to strained relationships. Conversely, spiritually aware individuals tend to foster compassion, understanding, and harmony in their interactions.

Throughout history and across various religious traditions, spiritual blindness has been a recurring theme. In Christianity, Jesus frequently rebuked the Pharisees for their inability to see the truth of His teachings despite their outward religiosity.

Similarly, in Buddhism, ignorance is considered a root cause of suffering. These perspectives underline the universal nature of spiritual blindness and the need for self-awareness and enlightenment.

Faith and self-reflection are vital tools for overcoming spiritual blindness. Faith acts as a guiding light, providing hope and direction. Reflection helps individuals recognize their shortcomings and realign their priorities. Practices such as meditation, prayer, and studying sacred texts can help one gain clarity and insight, breaking free from the chains of spiritual ignorance.

Community plays a crucial role in addressing spiritual blindness. Supportive relationships with spiritually aware individuals can help one recognize and overcome their blind spots. Spiritual mentors, religious leaders, and close friends can offer guidance, encouragement, and accountability. Engaging in collective worship or study sessions can also provide fresh perspectives and foster growth. In the modern world, spiritual blindness is exacerbated by distractions such as technology, consumerism, and the fast-paced nature of life.

Social media, for instance, often promotes comparison and superficiality, pulling people away from deeper connections and truths.

Recognizing these challenges is essential for maintaining spiritual clarity in an increasingly noisy and chaotic environment.

Attaining spiritual clarity brings profound rewards, such as inner peace, fulfillment, and a sense of purpose. Spiritually aware individuals are better equipped to navigate challenges, make wise decisions, and build meaningful relationships.

They find joy in simplicity and are more likely to contribute positively to the world around them. Spiritual blindness is a condition that affects many, but it is not irreversible. By acknowledging its causes, seeking guidance, and committing to practices that promote spiritual growth, individuals can overcome this blindness. The journey toward spiritual clarity is not always easy, but it is profoundly rewarding, leading to a life of purpose, peace, and deeper connection with the divine and with others.

CHAPTER 10:

SPIRITUAL PERCEPTION

Spiritual perception is the ability to discern deeper truths and recognize the presence of the divine in daily life. It goes beyond physical senses, tapping into an awareness of purpose, morality, and connection.

This heightened sense of perception allows individuals to navigate life with wisdom, compassion, and clarity. By exploring spiritual perception, we gain tools to lead more meaningful lives and foster harmony within ourselves and our communities. The roots of spiritual perception lie in openness and humility.

By setting aside preconceived notions and embracing curiosity, individuals create a fertile ground for spiritual growth. Practices like mindfulness, meditation, and prayer serve as gateways to a deeper understanding of oneself and the universe.

These foundations are essential for developing the ability to perceive and act on spiritual truths. Unlike logical reasoning, which is grounded in tangible evidence and analysis, spiritual perception operates in the realm of intuition and faith.

It does not seek to replace logic but to complement it by addressing the questions that logic cannot answer, such as the nature of existence and the purpose of life. Cultivating spiritual perception allows individuals to approach life's mysteries with a sense of wonder and openness. Faith is central to spiritual perception, acting as a bridge between the seen and unseen.

It provides the confidence to trust in truths that may not yet be fully understood. Through faith, individuals can overcome doubt and fear, paving the way for spiritual insights. Faith also fosters resilience, helping people find meaning and strength even in the face of challenges. Spiritual perception enhances empathy by fostering an understanding of the interconnectedness of all life.

Recognizing the divine in others encourages compassion and reduces judgment. This perspective enables individuals to build stronger, more meaningful relationships and to approach conflicts with a spirit of reconciliation and love. Historical and cultural perspectives on spiritual perception throughout history, spiritual perception has been celebrated in various cultures and religions.

In Hinduism, the concept of "darshan" refers to the ability to see and be seen by the divine. In Christianity, spiritual perception is often associated with the "eyes of the heart" mentioned in scripture. These traditions highlight the universal human quest for a deeper connection with the divine. Developing spiritual perception requires intentional effort and practice.

Techniques such as meditation, journaling, and studying sacred texts can deepen one's awareness. Spending time in nature and engaging in acts of service are also powerful ways to enhance spiritual perception.

The Inner Eye

These practices help individuals tune into their inner wisdom and align with their higher purpose. Modern life poses significant challenges to spiritual perception. Constant distractions, the pressure of material success, and skepticism can hinder one's ability to connect with deeper truths. Overcoming these challenges requires discipline, a supportive community, and a commitment to prioritizing spiritual growth over fleeting pleasures. Spiritual perception brings numerous benefits, including inner peace, clarity of purpose, and a sense of fulfillment.

It allows individuals to approach life with gratitude and resilience, transforming hardships into opportunities for growth. Moreover, it fosters a sense of unity and love, enriching relationships and contributing to a more harmonious world.

Spiritual perception is a profound gift that enables individuals to live with greater awareness and purpose. By cultivating this ability, we can overcome the limitations of the physical world and connect with deeper truths.

The journey toward spiritual perception is a lifelong process, but its rewards—peace, wisdom, and a sense of divine connection—are immeasurable.

CHAPTER 11:

EYES OF FAITH

The "eyes of faith" symbolize the ability to perceive spiritual truths and divine realities that transcend physical vision. This perspective allows individuals to see beyond appearances, embracing trust in the unseen and the eternal.

Understanding the eyes of faith equips one with the strength to navigate life's uncertainties and the wisdom to discern deeper meanings in everyday experiences. This chapter explores the significance, development, and transformative power of the eyes of faith. The eyes of faith teach us to trust in what is unseen, relying on the promises of a higher power rather than tangible evidence.

This trust requires a surrender of control, embracing a belief in divine providence. In a world dominated by skepticism and empiricism, faith invites individuals to lean on spiritual convictions, finding hope even when circumstances appear bleak. Doubt is a natural part of the human experience, yet the eyes of faith provide clarity and reassurance.

When faced with uncertainty, faith allows individuals to focus on the greater picture, trusting that challenges serve a higher purpose. This spiritual vision shifts attention from immediate struggles to the enduring promises of peace, purpose, and fulfillment. Through the eyes of faith, resilience emerges as a profound strength. Believers find courage to endure hardships, knowing that trials are temporary and often serve to refine character.

This resilience stems from an unshakable trust in divine support, enabling individuals to face adversity with grace and determination. The eyes of faith transform how individuals perceive others, encouraging a lens of compassion, forgiveness, and understanding. Recognizing the divine spark in each person fosters empathy and reduces judgment.

Faith challenges us to look beyond surface flaws, seeing the potential for growth and redemption in everyone. Throughout history, countless figures have demonstrated the power of the eyes of faith.

Biblical accounts, such as Abraham's trust in God's promises or Moses leading his people through the wilderness, highlight unwavering faith in divine guidance. These narratives inspire contemporary believers to cultivate similar trust and vision in their spiritual journeys. Developing the eyes of faith requires intentional spiritual practices. Regular prayer, meditation, and study of sacred texts help sharpen spiritual vision.

Acts of service and gratitude also enhance faith by fostering a deeper connection with the divine and an appreciation for life's blessings. These practices guide individuals toward a clearer, more faith-filled perspective. In today's fast-paced, materialistic society, maintaining the eyes of faith can be challenging.

Distractions, doubts, and the emphasis on tangible achievements often obscure spiritual vision. Overcoming these challenges involves creating space for reflection, seeking community support, and prioritizing spiritual growth over worldly pursuits. The eyes of faith have a profound transformative effect, fostering inner peace, hope, and a sense of purpose. This spiritual perspective empowers individuals to navigate life with confidence, embracing both joy and sorrow as part of a divine plan. Faithful vision also promotes unity, encouraging believers to contribute positively to the world around them. Living with the eyes of faith is a journey of trust, growth, and transformation.

By cultivating spiritual vision, individuals can rise above the limitations of the physical world, embracing a deeper connection with the divine. This perspective not only enriches personal lives but also inspires others to explore and embrace the boundless possibilities of faith.

CHAPTER 12:

THE VISION OF THE SEER

The "vision of the seer" refers to an extraordinary spiritual insight that transcends ordinary perception. Seers possess the ability to perceive divine truths, hidden realities, and the interconnectedness of all things. Their vision is not bound by time or physical limitations, allowing them to guide others toward enlightenment and clarity. This chapter delves into the nature of the seer's vision, exploring its origins, significance, and transformative potential.

The vision of the seer is rooted in a profound connection to the spiritual realm. It involves a heightened awareness that goes beyond the sensory world, offering a glimpse into divine will and purpose. This ability often requires purity of heart, deep meditation, and an unwavering commitment to truth.

Seers perceive the underlying harmony of creation, understanding the threads that weave together the physical and spiritual worlds. Throughout history, seers have served as spiritual guides, prophets, and visionaries. Their insights have shaped cultures, inspired movements, and provided solace in times of uncertainty.

By interpreting divine messages and revealing hidden truths, seers help individuals and communities align with their higher purpose. Their vision often serves as a beacon of hope, guiding humanity toward justice, compassion, and unity. The vision of the seer is not a product of mere human intellect but a gift from the divine. It emerges from a deep spiritual attune achieved through practices like prayer, fasting, and contemplation.

This connection enables seers to access wisdom beyond their own understanding, drawing from a wellspring of divine knowledge and love. The purity and humility of the seer play a crucial role in sustaining this gift. Seers often encounter significant challenges in their journey.

Their visions may be misunderstood, doubted, or rejected by those around them. The weight of divine revelation can also be burdensome, requiring immense courage and resilience.

Despite these difficulties, seers remain steadfast, trusting in the truth of their visions and their responsibility to share them with the world. Historical examples of seers' history is replete with examples of seers whose visions have transformed the world. Figures like Isaiah, who foresaw the coming of the Messiah, and Joan of Arc, who was guided by divine voices, demonstrate the profound impact of seer-like insight.

These individuals exemplify the power of spiritual vision to inspire faith, courage, and change, leaving an indelible mark on humanity. While the vision of the seer is often considered a rare gift, elements of it can be cultivated by anyone seeking spiritual growth. Practices such as mindfulness, meditation, and the study of sacred texts help sharpen spiritual perception.

Developing qualities like humility, patience, and openness to divine guidance also allows individuals to attune to the deeper truths of existence. In today's world, modern-day seers play a vital role in addressing contemporary challenges. Their vision helps bridge the gap between materialism and spirituality, offering guidance in navigating complex moral and existential dilemmas. By fostering awareness and encouraging collective growth, modern seers contribute to building a more compassionate and harmonious society.

The seer's vision has a transformative effect on those who encounter it. It inspires self-reflection, ignites faith, and encourages individuals to pursue their spiritual journey. By revealing hidden truths and divine purpose, the seer's vision empowers people to live with greater intention, resilience, and joy.

The vision of the seer is a profound gift that illuminates the path toward spiritual enlightenment and unity. By understanding and embracing this vision, individuals and communities can rise above mundane concerns and connect with the divine purpose of existence. Whether through the guidance of a seer or the cultivation of personal, spiritual insight, the journey toward clearer vision transforms lives and fosters a deeper connection to the eternal.

CHAPTER 13:

THE DANGER OF SPIRITUAL BLINDNESS

Spiritual blindness refers to the inability to perceive or understand spiritual truths and divine realities. It is a condition that affects the soul, clouding judgment and distorting one's view of purpose and connection with the divine. This blindness is not a lack of physical sight but a lack of spiritual insight, which can lead to confusion, moral decay, and separation from higher truths.

In this chapter, we will explore the causes, consequences, and remedies for spiritual blindness, as well as its impact on individuals and communities. Spiritual blindness often stems from pride, materialism, and a hardened heart. When individuals prioritize worldly achievements and pleasures over spiritual growth, they become disconnected from their inner selves and divine guidance. Other causes include ignorance of sacred teachings, trauma, and persistent doubt.

These factors create barriers that prevent individuals from seeing the bigger picture of life and their spiritual potential. Recognizing spiritual blindness is the first step toward overcoming it. Symptoms include a lack of compassion, an absence of purpose, and a tendency to judge others harshly. Individuals may also experience restlessness, dissatisfaction, or a feeling of being lost. These signs indicate a need to reconnect with the divine and seek clarity in one's spiritual journey. The consequences of spiritual blindness are profound and far-reaching. On a personal level, it leads to feelings of emptiness, fear, and despair.

In a broader context, it contributes to societal issues such as greed, injustice, and conflict. Without spiritual vision, individuals and communities lose sight of ethical principles and the interconnectedness of all life, resulting in division and suffering. Spiritual blindness often damages relationships by fostering misunderstandings, selfishness, and lack of empathy.

When individuals fail to see the divine in others, they become less forgiving and more prone to conflict.

This blindness hinders meaningful connections and undermines the foundation of trust and love in relationships. History provides numerous examples of spiritual blindness leading to devastating consequences. Events such as wars, persecution, and the exploitation of natural resources highlight humanity's failure to act with wisdom and compassion. These examples serve as warnings, emphasizing the importance of spiritual awareness in preventing similar mistakes in the future. Faith is a powerful antidote to spiritual blindness.

It opens the heart and mind to divine truths, fostering a sense of purpose and connection. Practices such as prayer, meditation, and community worship help individuals cultivate faith and regain spiritual sight. Through faith, individuals can transcend doubt and fear, embracing a vision of hope and love. Self-reflection is essential for overcoming spiritual blindness. By examining one's thoughts, actions, and beliefs, individuals can identify the barriers blocking their spiritual vision. This process requires humility, honesty, and a willingness to change. Self-reflection leads to greater self-awareness and a deeper connection with the divine.

Overcoming spiritual blindness is a journey that involves intentional practices and a commitment to growth. Regular engagement with sacred texts, acts of service, and seeking guidance from spiritual mentors are effective ways to cultivate clarity. This path requires patience and perseverance, but the rewards—peace, wisdom, and a sense of purpose—are immeasurable. The danger of spiritual blindness lies in its ability to obscure truth and disconnect individuals from their higher purpose.

However, by recognizing its causes and consequences, and actively seeking remedies, individuals can regain spiritual sight. Embracing spiritual clarity transforms lives, fostering deeper connections with others and the divine. In a world filled with distractions, the journey toward spiritual vision is both a challenge and a profound blessing.

CHAPTER 14:

CALL TO SPIRITUAL

AWAKENING

In a world driven by material pursuits and constant distractions, the call to spiritual awakening grows ever more urgent.

Spiritual awakening refers to a profound shift in consciousness, where individuals move beyond superficial concerns to embrace deeper truths about themselves, the universe, and the divine. It is a transformative process that renews purpose, fosters inner peace, and connects people to their higher selves.

This chapter explores the essence of spiritual awakening, its challenges, and the ways it enriches life for individuals and communities alike. Before awakening, many experience a state of spiritual dormancy marked by disconnection, confusion, and a lack of fulfillment. Symptoms include chasing external validation, feeling trapped in routines, and struggling to find meaning in life's experiences.

Recognizing these signs is the first step toward responding to the call for spiritual renewal. Spiritual awakening is often triggered by pivotal life events—both joyful and challenging. Loss, illness, or a sudden insight can serve as catalysts, shaking individuals from complacency and prompting them to seek higher understanding. At other times, the call emerges gradually, through persistent inner yearning or exposure to spiritual teachings. These moments of clarity invite people to begin their journey of transformation. The path to spiritual awakening is neither linear nor easy. It involves phases of self-discovery, shedding old beliefs, and embracing new perspectives. As individuals confront their fears and shadows, they often experience moments of doubt and struggle. Yet, these challenges are integral to growth, clearing the way for profound realizations and renewed purpose. Faith acts as a cornerstone for spiritual awakening. It provides the strength to endure uncertainties and trust in the journey ahead.

Practices such as meditation, prayer, and mindfulness play a crucial role in nurturing awareness and fostering connection with the divine. These disciplines anchor individuals, enabling them to navigate the complexities of awakening with grace.

Awakening to oneness, one of the most profound aspects of spiritual awakening, is the realization of oneness. This awareness dissolves the illusion of separation, revealing the interconnectedness of all life. It fosters compassion, empathy, and a sense of responsibility for others and the world. By embracing oneness, individuals find a deeper sense of belonging and purpose.

The journey of spiritual awakening is not without obstacles. Skepticism from others, fear of change, and the temptation to revert to old patterns can hinder progress. These challenges test one's commitment but overcoming them strengthens resolve and deepens spiritual insight. Support from mentors and spiritual communities often proves invaluable during these times. Spiritual awakening transforms not only individuals but also the societies they inhabit. Awakened individuals bring clarity, compassion, and creativity to their relationships and endeavors. They inspire others to embark on their own spiritual journeys, creating a ripple effect that fosters collective growth and harmony. Living an awakened life means integrating spiritual insights into daily actions.

It involves approaching challenges with wisdom, nurturing relationships with authenticity, and contributing to the greater good. This integration ensures that awakening is not a fleeting experience but a lasting transformation that shapes every aspect of life. The call to spiritual awakening is a profound invitation to live with greater awareness, purpose, and connection.

By heeding this call, individuals embark on a journey that enriches their lives and the lives of those around them. Awakening is not an end but a beginning—a continuous process of growth and discovery. In embracing this path, humanity moves closer to realizing its divine potential and creating a world rooted in love and understanding.

CHAPTER 15:

THE ROLE OF THE HOLY SPIRIT

The Holy Spirit is a central figure in many spiritual traditions, particularly within Christianity, where it is seen as the third person of the Trinity. Its role encompasses guidance, comfort, empowerment, and the illumination of divine truths. The Holy Spirit acts as a bridge between humanity and the divine, fostering a deeper connection with God and enabling transformative spiritual experiences.

This chapter delves into the multifaceted role of the Holy Spirit, its significance in daily life, and its transformative power in individuals and communities. One of the primary roles of the Holy Spirit is to guide individuals on their spiritual journeys.

It provides wisdom and discernment, helping believers navigate life's complexities and make decisions aligned with divine will. This guidance often comes through inner promptings, scripture, or the counsel of others inspired by the Spirit. By attuning to the Holy Spirit, individuals find clarity and direction in their lives. The Holy Spirit is also known as the Comforter, offering solace during trials and tribulations.

In moments of pain, loss, or uncertainty, the Spirit provides peace that transcends understanding. This comforting presence reminds individuals of God's unwavering love and reassures them that they are never alone. The Spirit's role as a Comforter strengthens faith and resilience, enabling believers to endure challenges with hope. The Holy Spirit empowers individuals to fulfill their divine purpose and serve others.

It grants spiritual gifts such as wisdom, prophecy, and healing, equipping believers for various roles in ministry and community service. This empowerment inspires courage, creativity, and compassion, enabling individuals to make meaningful contributions to the world and glorify God through their actions. The transformative power of the Holy Spirit is unparalleled.

It works within individuals to renew their minds, purify their hearts, and align their desires with THE divine principles. This inner transformation fosters spiritual growth, enabling believers to embody virtues such as love, humility, and patience. By yielding to the Spirit's work, individuals become more reflective of divine character.

The Holy Spirit unites believers, fostering harmony within communities of faith. It transcends differences, drawing people together in mutual love and understanding. This unity reflects the Spirit's role in building the body of Christ, where every member contributes to the collective mission. Through the Spirit, communities find strength in diversity and work together to advance God's kingdom.

The Holy Spirit plays a vital role in deepening prayer and worship. It intercedes on behalf of believers, expressing their deepest longings when words fail. The Spirit also inspires heartfelt worship, drawing individuals into a profound encounter with the divine. This dynamic involvement enhances the spiritual experience, making prayer and worship more meaningful and transformative. The Holy Spirit illuminates divine truths, making scripture and spiritual teachings come alive. It opens the eyes of believers to the mysteries of God, revealing insights that inspire faith and understanding. This revelatory role ensures that individuals grow in wisdom and remain rooted in truth. By relying on the Spirit, believers gain a deeper appreciation of God's word and will.

The Holy Spirit is not confined to extraordinary moments but is actively involved in the daily lives of believers. It provides strength, guidance, and inspiration in routine tasks and decisions. By cultivating an awareness of the Spirit's presence, individuals experience a sense of purpose and peace in every aspect of life. This constant companionship transforms ordinary days into opportunities for spiritual growth.

The role of the Holy Spirit is profound and transformative, touching every aspect of life and faith. From guiding and comforting to empowering and uniting, the Spirit acts as a divine presence that fosters growth, understanding, and connection. By with greater purpose, harmony, and spiritual vitality. In yielding to its influence, believers find a source of endless grace, wisdom, and love.

CHAPTER 16:

THE IMPORTANCE OF

DISCERNMENT

Discernment is the ability to distinguish between truth and falsehood, right and wrong, and the divine and the mundane. It is a spiritual skill that enables individuals to make wise decisions aligned with their values and higher purpose. In a world filled with conflicting information and moral ambiguity, discernment serves as a guiding light, helping people navigate life's complexities with clarity and integrity.

This chapter explores the essence of discernment, its significance, and how it can be cultivated for personal and communal growth. At its core, discernment is about making sound decisions that reflect wisdom and virtue.

It goes beyond mere logic or emotion, incorporating a spiritual awareness that seeks alignment with higher truths. Whether deciding on a career path, a relationship, or a moral dilemma, discernment ensures that choices are made with intentionality and foresight.

This ability prevents impulsive actions and fosters a life rooted in purpose and direction. Discernment is deeply spiritual, as it involves tuning into divine guidance and inner wisdom. This process often requires prayer, meditation, or quiet reflection to connect with the still, small voice within. By seeking spiritual insight, individuals can discern God's will or the universal principles that align with their faith or values. This spiritual dimension elevates discernment from a practical skill to a sacred practice. Without discernment, individuals risk falling prey to deception, manipulation, and poor choices. In today's fast-paced and information-saturated world, the absence of discernment can lead to confusion, conflict, and regret. A lack of this skill undermines personal growth and can have far-reaching consequences, from broken relationships to societal discord.

Recognizing the dangers of indiscriminate decision-making underscores the necessity of cultivating discernment. Discernment is closely tied to emotional intelligence, as it requires understanding and managing one's emotions to make balanced choices. By being aware of their emotional state, individuals can avoid reactive decisions and instead respond thoughtfully.

This connection highlights the interplay between intellect, emotion, and spirituality in the practice of discernment. Developing discernment is a lifelong journey that requires intentional practice. This includes studying sacred texts, seeking wise counsel, and reflecting on past experiences to glean lessons.

Additionally, practices such as mindfulness and journaling can sharpen one's ability to perceive patterns and make thoughtful decisions. Through consistent effort, individuals can strengthen their discernment and apply it to all areas of life. Discernment is not solely an individual endeavor; it is often enriched by the insights of others. Trusted friends, mentors, and spiritual leaders can provide valuable perspectives that clarify decision-making. Engaging with a community fosters collective wisdom and accountability, ensuring that discernment is grounded in diverse experiences and shared values. During crises, discernment becomes even more critical as emotions run high and stakes are elevated. In such moments, the ability to remain calm and seek divine or inner guidance can prevent hasty decisions. Discernment provides a steady anchor, enabling individuals to navigate uncertainty with confidence and composure. This resilience highlights the power of discernment in overcoming challenges.

The benefits of discernment are manifold, including greater peace of mind, deeper relationships, and a more fulfilling life. By making decisions that align with their true selves and higher purpose, individuals experience a sense of harmony and satisfaction.

The rewards extend beyond personal well-being, as discernment also contributes to ethical leadership and societal progress. Discernment is an invaluable skill that shapes every aspect of life, from personal choices to broader societal impact.

By embracing discernment, individuals cultivate wisdom, integrity, and spiritual depth.

This practice not only enriches their own lives but also inspires others to act with clarity and purpose. In a world where guidance is often needed, the importance of discernment cannot be overstated, as it illuminates the path to truth, virtue, and fulfillment.

CHAPTER 17:

THE EYE OF THE HEART

The phrase "the eye of the heart" symbolizes an inner capacity to perceive spiritual truths beyond the limitations of physical senses. This concept appears in various spiritual traditions and emphasizes the importance of intuition, faith, and deep inner awareness. Unlike the eyes of the body, the eye of the heart sees the invisible—love, hope, and divine presence.

This chapter delves into the meaning of the eye of the heart, its role in spiritual growth, and how one can nurture this profound way of seeing. The heart is often regarded as more than just a physical organ; it is seen as the seat of the soul and a vessel for divine connection. In many traditions, the heart represents the center of love, compassion, and wisdom. The eye of the heart refers to this deeper dimension of perception, enabling individuals to discern spiritual realities that remain hidden to the physical eye.

This perspective transforms the heart into a gateway to higher understanding. The ability to see with the eye of the heart does not come automatically; it requires awakening and cultivation. This awakening begins with introspection, prayer, and a sincere desire to seek the truth. Practices such as meditation, silence, and mindful living help remove the veils that obscure the heart's vision. By quieting the mind and opening the heart, individuals become more receptive to divine insights. The eye of the heart is closely linked to intuition, which is the innate ability to sense truths beyond rational analysis. Intuition acts as a spiritual compass, guiding individuals toward decisions that resonate with their higher purpose. By trusting the subtle guidance of the heart, people can navigate life with greater confidence and alignment with divine will.

Love and compassion are essential to the functioning of the eye of the heart. When the heart is filled with love, it perceives the inherent beauty and worth in all things. Compassion enables individuals to see beyond surface level differences and connect with the shared humanity of others. This perspective fosters empathy, unity, and a deeper sense of purpose. Faith plays a vital role in activating the eye of the heart.

Faith involves trusting in unseen realities and embracing the mysteries of the divine. This trust allows individuals to transcend doubt and fear, enabling the heart's vision to flourish. Faith acts as a bridge between the known and the unknown, grounding spiritual perception in unwavering belief. The eye of the heart can be clouded by ego, fear, and materialism. These obstacles prevent individuals from accessing their deeper wisdom and spiritual insights. Overcoming these barriers requires self-awareness and intentional effort.

Practices such as forgiveness, gratitude, and humility help cleanse the heart and restore its clarity of vision.

THE TRANSFORMATIVE POWER OF HEART VISION

Seeing with the eye of the heart is transformative, reshaping how individuals perceive themselves, others, and the world. This perspective nurtures a sense of awe, gratitude, and interconnectedness.

It encourages people to live with authenticity and to approach challenges with courage and grace. The transformative power of heart vision fosters both personal and collective growth.

CULTIVATING THE EYE OF THE HEART IN DAILY LIFE

Cultivating the eye of the heart is not limited to spiritual practices; it extends into everyday life. Acts of kindness, mindfulness, and intentional living help keep the heart's vision active and vibrant.

By approaching daily interactions with love and awareness, individuals can maintain a heart-centered perspective that enriches their lives and those around them. Conclusion: embracing the heart's vision, the eye of the heart offers a profound way of seeing that transcends physical limitations and reveals the deeper truths of existence.

By awakening and cultivating this inner vision, individuals can experience greater clarity, connection, and purpose. Embracing the heart's vision transforms lives, fostering a world rooted in love, compassion, and spiritual wisdom. This way of

The Inner Eye

seeing is not merely a gift but a calling to live with deeper awareness and divine alignment.

CHAPTER 18:

A CALL TO HUMILITY

Humility is a virtue often extolled but rarely understood in its depth and significance. It is not about self-deprecation or weakness but a profound recognition of one's place in the grand tapestry of existence. Humility allows individuals to approach life with grace, open-mindedness, and an unshakable sense of purpose. This chapter explores the multifaceted nature of humility, its role in fostering spiritual growth, and how embracing this virtue can lead to a life of deeper meaning and connection.

Contrary to misconceptions, humility is not a sign of weakness but a source of immense strength. It takes courage to admit limitations, acknowledge mistakes, and seek guidance. This strength is rooted in self-awareness and the ability to prioritize the greater good over personal pride. Through humility, individuals build resilience, navigate challenges with grace, and inspire others with their authenticity. Humility involves acknowledging the vastness of the divine and one's finite role within it.

This recognition fosters a sense of awe and reverence for life's mysteries and the Creator's wisdom. By understanding their dependence on a higher power, individuals cultivate gratitude and trust in divine providence, allowing them to surrender their egos and embrace a spirit of service. In relationships, humility manifests as the ability to listen, empathize, and prioritize others' needs. It encourages open communication and the willingness to admit faults, fostering deeper connections. Humble individuals create harmonious environments where respect and understanding flourish, strengthening bonds and building lasting relationships. Spiritual growth requires a humble heart that is open to learning and transformation. Humility enables individuals to accept divine guidance, embrace change, and seek forgiveness.

It dissolves the barriers of pride and self-righteousness, creating space for personal and spiritual renewal. Through humility, believers draw closer to their faith and uncover their true purpose. Pride and arrogance are obstacles to humility, often stemming from insecurity or an inflated sense of self. Overcoming these traits requires introspection, self-discipline, and a commitment to growth.

By practicing gratitude, seeking feedback, and focusing on other's well-being, individuals can dismantle the ego and embrace humility as a way of life.

Effective leadership is grounded in humility. Humble leaders prioritize the needs of their team, listen to diverse perspectives, and lead by example. They inspire trust and loyalty by demonstrating integrity and a willingness to learn. This approach creates environments of collaboration and innovation, benefiting both individuals and organizations. Humility is not confined to grand gestures; it is cultivated through daily actions and attitudes. Simple practices such as expressing gratitude, admitting mistakes, and valuing other's contributions reinforce humility. By approaching each day with a spirit of service and mindfulness, individuals can integrate humility into every aspect of their lives.

Living with humility brings profound rewards, including inner peace, deeper relationships, and a greater sense of purpose. Humility allows individuals to let go of unnecessary burdens, focus on what truly matters, and align their lives with their values. The humble life is one of fulfillment, harmony, and lasting impact.

The call to humility is an invitation to live authentically, embrace growth, and connect with the divine. It challenges individuals to rise above pride and selfishness, fostering a life of service, gratitude, and purpose. By answering this call, people not only transform their own lives but also inspire others to cultivate a more compassionate and harmonious world. Humility is not merely a virtue to aspire to but a way of being that enriches every facet of existence.

CHAPTER 19:

THE TRANSFORMATIVE POWER

OF SIGHT

Sight is a gift that extends far beyond the physical act seeing. It represents perception, understanding, and insight—a way of interacting with the world that can shape our lives in profound ways.

The transformative power of sight lies not only in what we observe with our eyes but in how we interpret, respond to, and grow from these observations. This chapter explores the deeper dimensions of sight, both literal and metaphorical, and its potential to bring about personal and spiritual transformation.

Sight functions on two interconnected levels: the physical and the spiritual. Physically, sight allows us to navigate the world, experience beauty, and connect with others. Spiritually, it enables us to perceive deeper truths and align with higher purposes. The interplay between these dimensions enriches our understanding of life, teaching us to value what is visible while seeking meaning in the unseen.

Clarity of sight begins with awareness—a conscious effort to observe without judgment or bias. This practice involves seeing the world as it is, rather than through the lens of preconceived notions or expectations. Awareness cultivates mindfulness, which sharpens both our physical and spiritual vision. Through clarity, individuals gain a deeper appreciation for life's intricacies and discover new paths of growth. Perspective shapes how we interpret what we see. A shift in perspective can transform challenges into opportunities and pain into lessons. By viewing life through a lens of gratitude and possibility, individuals harness the transformative power of sight to overcome obstacles and embrace growth.

This ability to reframe experiences is a cornerstone of resilience and wisdom. True sight involves seeing with compassion-recognizing the humanity in others and understanding their struggles.

Compassionate sight breaks down barriers, fostering empathy and connection. By choosing to see the world through compassionate eyes, individuals contribute to a culture of kindness and mutual respect, creating ripples of positive change. Sometimes, the most critical truths are overlooked because they cannot be seen with the eyes. Spiritual blindness—an inability to perceive meaning, purpose, or divinity—can hinder personal growth and fulfillment.

Overcoming this blindness requires introspection, humility, and a willingness to open the heart to deeper truths. Sight has the power to inspire change, both within and around us. Visionaries—those who see beyond the present and imagine a better future—harness this power to lead movements, innovate solutions, and transform communities. Each individual possesses the potential to be a visionary by aligning their sight with their values and aspirations. Faith nurtures vision by providing a framework for seeing beyond the immediate and the tangible. It encourages individuals to trust in the unseen and to seek guidance from higher powers. Faith expands the boundaries of sight, enabling people to perceive possibilities and embrace their purpose with confidence and conviction. Reflection sharpens our sight by allowing us to process and learn from our experiences. Taking time to contemplate what we see—both physically and spiritually—provides clarity and insight. Reflection fosters growth, helping individuals align their actions with their values and aspirations.

The transformative power of sight lies in its ability to shape our perceptions, decisions, and connections. By embracing sight in all its dimensions—physical, spiritual, and metaphorical—individuals can unlock new levels of understanding, compassion, and purpose. Sight is not merely a sense but a profound gift, offering endless opportunities for growth and transformation. To see truly is to live fully, with eyes and heart wide open to the beauty and potential of life.

CHAPTER 20:

THE POWER OF PRAYER

Prayer is a universal practice that transcends cultures, religions, and traditions, serving as a vital bridge between humanity and the divine. It is an act of communication, devotion, and surrender, allowing individuals to express gratitude, seek guidance, and find solace. The power of prayer lies in its ability to transform hearts, strengthen faith, and bring about profound changes in both individuals and their circumstances. This chapter explores the multifaceted nature of prayer, its spiritual and emotional impact, and how it can be a source of transformation and connection.

Prayer is more than recitation; it is an intimate dialogue with the divine. Whether silent or spoken, formal or spontaneous, prayer reflects the deepest yearnings of the soul. It is an act of humility and trust, acknowledging the presence of a higher power.

The nature of prayer varies widely, yet its essence remains the same: a heartfelt connection with the divine, rooted in sincerity and faith.

In moments of despair, uncertainty, or difficulty, prayer serves as a wellspring of strength. By turning to prayer, individuals find reassurance and a sense of peace that transcends their immediate struggles. This strength arises not only from the act of praying but also from the belief that they are supported and guided by a higher power. Prayer empowers individuals to face challenges with courage and resilience.

Gratitude is a powerful element of prayer, capable of transforming perspectives and attitudes. By expressing thanks, individuals shift their focus from what they lack to the blessings they have. Gratitude filled prayers foster contentment, humility, and joy, cultivating a mindset of abundance and appreciation. This transformative effect extends beyond prayer, enriching daily interactions and relationships.

One of the most profound aspects of prayer is intercession— praying on behalf of others. Intercessory prayer embodies compassion, empathy, and selflessness, allowing individuals to share in others' joys and burdens. This practice not only strengthens communal bonds but also deepens the spiritual lives of those who engage in it, reminding them of the interconnectedness of all beings.

The act of prayer often brings a sense of inner peace, calming the mind and soothing the soul. This peace arises from surrendering worries and placing trust in the divine. Regular prayer fosters a state of serenity that helps individuals navigate life's uncertainties with grace and composure. Through prayer, they find a sanctuary where they can rest, reflect, and rejuvenate. Prayer provides clarity and direction in times of confusion or indecision. By seeking divine guidance, individuals open themselves to insights and wisdom that transcend their understanding. This guidance often comes in subtle forms—a feeling, a thought, or an opportunity—leading them toward paths aligned with their purpose and values. When practiced collectively, prayer becomes a powerful force for unity and transformation. Group prayer strengthens relationships, fosters solidarity, and amplifies its spiritual impact. It reminds participants of their shared humanity and common aspirations, creating a sense of belonging and mutual support. Faith is both the foundation and the fruit of prayer.

Through prayer, individuals deepen their trust in the divine and affirm their beliefs. This trust empowers them to face life's uncertainties with hope and confidence, knowing that they are guided and supported. The synergy between faith and prayer creates a cycle of spiritual growth and renewal. The power of prayer lies not only in its ability to connect individuals with the divine but also in its transformative impact on their hearts, minds, and lives. Prayer nurtures faith, fosters gratitude, and strengthens resilience, offering solace and guidance in every circumstance. By embracing prayer as a daily practice, individuals can cultivate a deeper sense of purpose, peace, and connection, living a life enriched by the presence of the divine.

CHAPTER 21:

EMPATHY AND COMPASSION

Empathy and compassion are the cornerstones of meaningful human interaction and understanding. These virtues enable individuals to bridge gaps, foster unity, and create a more harmonious world. Empathy allows us to understand and share in another's feelings, while compassion inspires action to alleviate suffering.

Together, they form a powerful duo that can transform relationships, communities, and even global dynamics. This chapter delves into the profound importance of empathy and compassion, exploring their roles, benefits, and ways to cultivate them in everyday life.

Empathy is the ability to step into someone else's shoes and feel their emotions as if they were your own. It is not merely sympathy, which acknowledges another's plight from a distance, but an immersive experience that fosters deep understanding. Empathy requires active listening, an open heart, and a willingness to set aside one's judgments.

It is the foundation of emotional intelligence and a vital skill for navigating the complexities of human relationships. While empathy is about feeling with others, compassion takes it a step further by motivating action. Compassion compels individuals to alleviate pain and suffering, offering kindness and support without expecting anything in return. This transformative power of compassion has been the driving force behind countless acts of selflessness and heroism, demonstrating humanity's capacity for goodness and care. Healthy relationships thrive on empathy and compassion. These qualities enable individuals to communicate effectively, resolve conflicts, and build trust.

By understanding each other's perspectives and offering support during challenging times, people can strengthen their bonds and foster deeper connections. Empathy and compassion are the glue that holds relationships together, creating a foundation of mutual respect and understanding. Empathy and compassion are not innate traits reserved for a select few; they are skills that can be nurtured and developed.

Practices such as mindful listening, perspective-taking, and expressing gratitude can enhance one's ability to empathize. Similarly, engaging in acts of kindness, volunteering, and reflecting on shared humanity can cultivate compassion. These practices not only benefit others but also enrich one's own life.

Leadership rooted in empathy and compassion inspires loyalty, collaboration, and innovation. Empathetic leaders understand their team's needs and challenges, fostering an environment of trust and cooperation. Compassionate leadership goes beyond understanding, taking steps to support and uplift others. This approach not only enhances organizational success but also creates a culture of care and inclusivity. Scientific research reveals that empathy and compassion are deeply rooted in human biology.

Brain imaging studies show that specific neural networks activate when individuals observe or share in others' emotions. These findings underscore the natural capacity for empathy and highlight the importance of nurturing this ability. Understanding the neuroscience behind these virtues can inspire intentional efforts to practice and promote them. In a world often marked by division and conflict, empathy and compassion are vital for healing and unity. These qualities enable individuals to see beyond differences, fostering dialogue and mutual respect.

By approaching others with understanding and kindness, people can bridge cultural, political, and social divides, paving the way for a more harmonious and inclusive society. The practice of empathy and compassion offers numerous benefits, both for individuals and communities. On a personal level, these virtues enhance emotional well-being, reduce stress, and foster a sense of purpose. Collectively, they strengthen social bonds, create supportive networks, and contribute to a more compassionate world. The ripple effect of these practices can transform lives and inspire positive change on a broader scale. Empathy and compassion are not just ideals to aspire to but essential practices for a fulfilling and harmonious life.

They remind us of our shared humanity and the profound impact of understanding and kindness. By embracing these virtues, individuals can create deeper connections, inspire change, and contribute to a world where care and respect prevail. The journey toward greater empathy and compassion begins with a single step— a willingness to see, feel, and act with love.

CHAPTER 22:

INTERCONNECTEDNESS OF

CREATION

The world we inhabit is an intricate tapestry of interconnectedness, where every element of creation—from the smallest microorganism to the vast expanse of the cosmos—is interdependent. Recognizing this interconnectedness fosters a deeper respect for life and a sense of responsibility for preserving the delicate balance of nature. This chapter explores the profound ways in which all creation is linked, emphasizing the importance of harmony, stewardship, and understanding in maintaining the beauty and functionality of the natural world.

THE UNITY OF ALL LIVING THINGS

At the heart of creation lies the unity of all living things. Every organism, no matter how small, plays a role in sustaining the ecosystem. Plants provide oxygen, animals contribute to pollination and seed dispersal, and microorganisms break down organic matter to enrich the soil.

This interconnected web demonstrates reliance each species has on another, highlighting the necessity of preserving biodiversity for the health of the planet.

THE ROLE OF HUMANS IN CREATION

Humans occupy a unique position within the interconnected web of creation. With advanced cognitive abilities and innovative potential, humanity has the power to nurture or disrupt the natural balance. This duality places a responsibility on individuals and societies to act as stewards of the Earth, ensuring that human activities support rather than harm the interconnected systems that sustain life. Ecosystems are a testament to the interconnectedness of creation. Forests, oceans, wetlands, and grasslands all function as complex networks where every organism has a role.

The removal or decline of one species can create cascading effects, disrupting the entire system. Understanding and protecting these ecosystems is crucial for maintaining the planet's health and resilience against environmental challenges. Many spiritual traditions emphasize the interconnectedness of creation as a reflection of divine wisdom and purpose.

From indigenous beliefs that honor the sacredness of nature to religious teachings that view humanity as caretakers of the Earth, spirituality often reinforces the idea that all life is interconnected. This perspective encourages reverence, gratitude, and humility in the face of nature's wonders. Human actions, both positive and negative, have far reaching effects on the interconnected web of creation. Pollution, deforestation, and overconsumption disrupt ecosystems, while conservation efforts, sustainable practices, and technological innovations can restore balance.

Acknowledging the impact of our choices empowers individuals and communities to act in ways that protect and enhance the natural world. The interconnectedness of creation offers valuable lessons about unity, cooperation, and balance. Observing nature's systems reveals the importance of working together and respecting limits. These lessons can be applied to human relationships, encouraging collaboration and mutual support in achieving shared goals.

Nature serves as a teacher, reminding humanity of the power of unity and interdependence. Science and technology play a crucial role in understanding and preserving the interconnectedness of creation. Advances in fields such as ecology, genetics, and environmental science shed light on the complex relationships within ecosystems.

Technology can also provide solutions for conservation, renewable energy, and sustainable development, helping humanity live in harmony with the natural world. Recognizing the interconnectedness of creation inspires a commitment to sustainability. By adopting practices that prioritize renewable resources, reduce waste, and minimize ecological footprints, individuals and societies can contribute to a healthier planet. A sustainable future depends on collective efforts to respect and nurture the delicate balance of life. The interconnectedness of creation is a profound reminder of the unity and balance inherent in the natural world. By understanding and respecting this interconnectedness, humanity can foster a deeper connection to life and take meaningful steps to protect the planet. Embracing the web of life not only ensures the well-being of future generations but also enriches our sense of purpose and belonging in a vast, interdependent universe.

CHAPTER 23:

CONCLUSION

The journey through the pages of this book has been one of introspection and revelation, illuminating the profound role of the "inner eye" in shaping our understanding of self, others, and the greater universe. The inner eye represents the seat of spiritual insight, discernment, and awareness—a perspective that transcends the physical realm and delves into the deeper truths of existence.

Throughout the chapters, we explored how spiritual blindness can obscure this vision, how prayer and humility sharpen its focus, and how empathy, compassion, and interconnectedness serve as pathways to enlightenment. These insights underscore the importance of cultivating an inner eye attuned to harmony, truth, and divine purpose. To truly embrace the vision of the inner eye is to recognize the interconnectedness of creation, the sanctity of life, and the responsibility we hold as stewards of this world. It compels us to act with integrity, love, and wisdom, transforming not only our personal journeys but also the collective experience of humanity.

The Inner Eye

May this book serve as a guide, a reflection, and an inspiration for those seeking clarity and depth in their spiritual journeys. May your inner eye remain open, ever seeking, and ever seeing.

ABOUT THE AUTHORS

Bishop Philip Harrison, DD, ThD., is a dedicated pastor, church planter, and global ministry leader, committed to spreading the gospel and empowering believers through prayer. He is the founder of Covenant Prayer Ministries in Jesus Christ, Inc. (CPM) and serves as pastor of little White Chapel, Philadelphia, Inc, fostering a strong faith community through worship and service. His ministry extends internationally as a co-founder of Universal Success Assembly, Inc.- Liberia, and The Light of Jesus Christ Ministry, Inc., both dedicated to evangelism and community support. A respected member of the College of Bishops, he collaborates with faith leaders to uphold sound doctrine.

Bishop Harrison holds a Doctor of Divinity from Sure Foundation Theological Institute and a Doctorate in Eschatology from Jameson School of Ministry and Theology, Philadelphia. Through his leadership, he continues to inspire and uplift countless lives.

~

Reverend Abraham K. Mulbah, DBS. is a Servant Leader who serves as an Assistant Pastor at The Fellowship of Intercessors in Philadelphia, Pennsylvania. Rev. Mulbah is married to Mrs. Hawa

Kamara Mulbah, and they are blessed with wonderful children in the USA, Canada, Africa and around the world. Reverend Mulbah is also the Senior Pastor and founder of The Greater Love International Ministries and The Greater Love International Christian Academy in Liberia, West Africa. TO GOD BE THE GLORY FOR THIS WONDERFUL BOOK!

www.ingramcontent.com/pod-product-compliance
Lightning Source LLC
Chambersburg PA
CBHW070016110426
42741CB00034B/1974